TABLE OF

C000243377

INTRODUCTION .... ‑

So, How Can I Help? .... - 2 -

How Do I Get Started? .... - 3 -

KITCHEN .... - 5 -

Shopping for Food .... - 5 -

Preparing And Cooking Meals .... - 9 -

Storing Food .... - 10 -

Washing Up Utensils .... - 11 -

Using a Dishwasher .... - 13 -

Cleaning The Kitchen .... - 14 -

Laundry .... - 15 -

Kitchen Roll .... - 19 -

BATHROOM .... - 20 -

Hair Care .... - 21 -

Hair Ties and Hair Styling Products .... - 24 -

Dry Shampoo .... - 25 -

Cotton Buds .... - 26 -

Shower Gel and Hand Soap .... - 26 -

Bathroom Accessories .... - 27 -

Bath Products .... - 29 -

Body Lotions .... - 29 -

Skin Care Products .... - 30 -

Razors and Shaving .... - 36 -

Natural Deodorants .... - 42 -

TOILET PAPER .... - 43 -

WET WIPES .... - 44 -

CLEANING THE BATHROOM .... - 44 -

MENSTRUAL PRODUCTS .... - 46 -

OUT & ABOUT .... - 48 -

FOOD AND DRINK .... - 48 -

SUN CREAM .... - 52 -

PLASTERS AND MEDICINES .... - 53 -

PARENTING .... - 54 -

PREPARING FOR YOUR LITTLE ONE .... - 54 -

NAPPIES AND WET WIPES .... - 57 -

BABY BOTTLES AND DUMMIES .... - 60 -

BABY FOOD .... - 61 -

CLEANING .... - 62 -

NATURAL CLEANING PRODUCTS .... - 62 -

SPONGES AND CLOTHS .... - 66 -

OTHER CHANGES .... - 68 -

CONCLUSION .... - 76 -

BIBLIOGRAPHY I

Sustainable Sal - Your Go-To Guide For Greener Living

Sally Brown

Tips and Advice for A More Sustainable and Eco-Conscious Lifestyle

Published by Eco-Sal   **eco-sal.co.uk/contact**

A resource page that contains links to support this book can be found using the QR code or website link below. Any words in green throughout the book have a corresponding link on this page

eco-sal.co.uk/rp1

INTRODUCTION

Unfortunately, we are living in a time where a linear economy is the norm - where raw materials are transformed into single use products and thrown away. It is estimated that around 50% of plastic is used just once before being discarded (Plasticoceans.org, 2021). This 'throwaway' culture has been causing destruction to our wildlife, our waters and our health, and yet we are still being convinced that convenience is what we need.

If we watch the adverts on television and see the ads that pop up when scrolling through social media, nine times out of ten they are telling us we need something because what we have already isn't good enough. We NEED the latest new gadget, even if our old one is working perfectly fine because the new model has a few more megapixels on the camera, or we NEED to have disposable cutlery at our party on Saturday night because washing up is an inconvenience.

What we are failing to realise is that 'away' does not exist. When we throw something 'away' it has to go somewhere. And the problem is, where things are constantly being made, used and put in the bin, we are piling up a HUGE amount of waste

- more than the planet can handle. The majority of this waste doesn't get recycled, but ends up in landfill, or worse, in the sea where it kills our marine life, damaging the environment for many years to come.

It has also become normal for us to use products that contain harsh chemicals in our homes and on our bodies. This not only has an adverse effect on our health but is also damaging to the environment and our precious ecosystems; the consequences of which are yet to be fully understood.

Here are some scary facts about plastic waste: (Plasticoceans.org, 2021)

- Less than 9% of all plastic gets recycled
- 10 million tons of plastic are dumped in the ocean every year
- 1 million marine animals are killed annually by plastic pollution
- Humans eat over 40 pounds of plastic in their lifetime

SO, HOW CAN I HELP

A lot of people have the opinion that there is "no point trying because one person on their own is not going to make a difference". I can completely understand this mindset because I used to have it myself. The truth is, there are so many others out there that are facing the same dilemma. If everyone made a small change here and there, change would happen!

There is also a misconception that living an eco-friendly lifestyle will break the bank. The fact is a lot of the alternatives out there don't have to cost a penny and can actually save you money in the long run!

I have written this book to show you how easy it can be to make changes to your lifestyle; changes that not only help the environment, but which I am confident will also have a positive effect on you and your family's health.

This is your go-to guide which you can refer to whilst on your journey to greener living. It is, in effect, your 'Eco-Pal'.

HOW DO I GET STARTED

As much as I'm sure we'd all like to, we won't go straight to being 100% plastic free overnight. It is a journey which isn't always an easy one. There are likely to be hurdles along the way, but we can do this! Every small change makes a difference. Below are some tips to help you get started on reducing your usage of single use plastics:

- Start with the easy stuff - things that don't affect your habits at all.
- Look at rooms inside your home and see where you use single use plastic (check out the rest of the book for things you can change in each area of the house and other areas of your life). Check out The Ultimate Plastic Free Project if you want a tool to help you do this.

- When you've established your list, you don't have to go out and buy replacements for all of it straight away. Start small and work your way up.
- The most important one - Don't throw away all of your plastic items that can still be used to buy a plastic free alternative!
- Before you swap, use up what you have or reuse/repurpose, before buying new wherever possible.

For this book, I have created a resource page with links to a variety of product examples and relevant websites for your reference (items identified with green font).

eco-sal.co.uk/rp1

I hope this helps. Enjoy reading!

KITCHEN

First things first - think of all of the things that are connected to your kitchen. These are the things I can think of: Purchase the food that you store in your kitchen, prepare and cook meals, wash up/clean dishes in a dishwasher, clean the kitchen, laundry, use a tumble dryer, use kitchen roll ... This isn't an exhaustive list. I have gone through each of these sections below:

SHOPPING FOR FOOD

Going back to the convenience thing, it has become the norm to just pop to the supermarket to get everything we need for the week's food shop in one go. I do see the appeal, but this is a culture which you may want to change as you become more environmentally conscious; one that may also save you some money!

Shop Seasonal

Shopping for fruit and vegetables that are in season means that you eat foods when they are naturally ready to harvest. This not only saves CO_2 emissions as the food then doesn't have to be shipped in from all over the world, but it also tends to be cheaper and tastes better as it is fresher. What's not to like with this swap?

To help you plan your meals, check out Hubbub.org which tells you what food is in season each month. (Hubbub.org, n.d.)

Support Local Businesses

If you have local greengrocers, farmers markets, and farm shops, try to shop for your groceries in these as it then keeps money in your local economy instead of giving your money to large corporations. Plus, it is then supporting small businesses who, especially during the current climate with the COVID pandemic, might need the money more than your local supermarket.

Also, if you have a local refill store near you, these shops tend to stock everything from refillable body wash and shampoo, to laundry detergent, to cereals and pasta. Just take your containers such as glass jars, reused plastic containers and bottles, and reusable shopping bags, and just fill them up with what you need. This eliminates the packaging waste which in most supermarkets, is plastic.

Buy Loose Fruit and Vegetables

Whether you choose to shop in your local greengrocers or at the supermarket, most places are now starting to offer more and more loose fruit and vegetables. Hopefully in the near future, it will become the norm and it will be unusual to see pre-packed groceries.

You don't need to use the single-use plastic bags that supermarkets provide. You can either make up a produce bag to use if you're feeling crafty, out of an old pillowcase or some material that you have around the house or look for some readymade alternatives. These can be used to buy your loose fruit and vegetables.

If you have to buy fruit and vegetables in plastic packaging, some supermarkets are now accepting these plastic bags in their recycling points for carrier bags. My local supermarket accepts the following so it's worth double checking what yours will accept.

- All carrier bags
- Bread bags
- Cereal bags
- Bags and wrappings used for fruits, vegetables, salads and flowers
- Bottle and can multipack wrapping
- Biscuit and cake wrappers
- Toilet roll & kitchen roll wrapping
- Rice and dry food wrappers

- Cheese wrappers
- Frozen food bags
- Household item wrapping
- Clothing bags
- Magazine and newspaper wrappers

Milk Deliveries

Milk from the supermarket comes in plastic bottles which are made from a plastic accepted by most kerbside recycling programs.

Whilst this is good, remember that less than 9% of plastics are actually recycled (Plasticoceans.org, 2021) so it is always better to reduce and reuse before relying on recycling.

Milk & More is a UK milk delivery company that also deliver a number of other groceries. They deliver milk in glass bottles that they then collect after use, clean and reuse for more milk deliveries. If you want to go one better, they are now offering oat milk in returnable glass bottles. Oat milk has a much better environmental footprint than cow's milk as it uses a lot less water, land and CO_2 to produce.

If you want a bit of a challenge and want to save a bit of money, you could also have a go at making your own oat milk using the recipe below which I found from a Google search - others are available (Minimalist Baker, n.d.):

- Add 1 cup rolled oats + 4 cups water to a high-speed blender Blend on high for 30-45 seconds
- Strain through a clean t-shirt or towel twice.
- To make use of the oat milk pulp, why not make some oat cookies so that it doesn't go to waste?

PREPARING AND COOKING MEALS

Generic Pointers for Cooking

- When your chopping boards and cooking utensils break or are at the end of their useful life, opt for sustainable wooden or metal utensils instead of plastic ones.

- If you need foil for cooking, after use, wash the foil off so that it is clean and roll it up in a ball. Keep adding to the ball when you use foil, and when the ball is roughly the size of your fist, you can put this in the recycling bin. It needs to be big enough to be picked up by the sorting machines at the recycling centre.

- Microwaves use up to 80% less energy than an oven (Energy.gov, 2014) so if you need to heat something up, go for the microwave first.

- When you've boiled rice or pasta, the starchy water can be used to water your houseplants (once cooled) instead of using fresh water.

- Batch cook so that you can just heat up meals the next day for lunches or for future meals. You can reuse plastic containers or silicone pouches to store the meals in the fridge/freezer.

Composting

Putting all of your organic food scraps into a compost bin is a great way to reduce your waste going to landfill. You can put things like fruit and vegetable scraps, egg shells, wood, gardening waste and plastic free tea bags in a compost bin. Bins can be found cheaply, and some of them can take a little bit of caring for, but I found a short beginners guide if you are new to the concept.

You can also get a Bokashi compost bin which is an indoor bin. Bokashi is a fermentation process which produces a highly nutritious plant food and fertiliser tea (Wiggly Wigglers, 2020). The difference between this and normal composting is that you can put pretty much all organic waste in there, including meat, therefore saving more waste from going to landfill. This does involve a little bit of work, and also requires purchasing a Bokashi bran to assist with the fermentation process.

STORING FOOD

How do you store leftovers and sandwiches for the next day? If you currently rely on single-use cling film and aluminium foil, don't fret. Here are a few eco-friendly alternatives that you can opt for:

- Reuse old take-away containers to store food in
- Put leftovers in a bowl and cover with beeswax wraps or silicone lids
- For your sandwiches, you can get reusable sandwich wraps to take your lunch out with you.

WASHING UP UTENSILS

Washing Up Liquid

You can easily reduce your plastic use by opting for a washing-up soap bar. The bars last ages and cut through grease and grime, just as Fairy liquid would do. The only difference is instead of putting the product in the water to make bubbles, you use it directly on the item being washed by wiping your sponge over the soap bar first. Alternatively, you can use Multi-Purpose Sheets which you pop into the water whilst it's running to create the usual bubbles.

If you fancy a challenge, you can easily make your own washing up liquid using an essential oil fragrance of your choice. There are lots of recipes online, but I have added one to the Resource Page that I have found for your reference that includes things you might already have in your cupboard (Jo, 2006). You can then decant your homemade washing up liquid into an old plastic bottle to keep reusing.

Washing Up Brushes and Sponges

Did you know that plastic washing up sponges emit micro-plastics as they wear? This is a scary thought considering how frequently we use them! That's a crazy amount of plastic going down the drain and affecting marine life.

Here are a few alternatives you can use in place of plastic sponges, scourers and brushes for your washing up. All are made from natural materials that are free from plastic and will biodegrade:

- Tough None Sponge - Made from cotton, bamboo and hessian
- Eco Coconut Scourers - Made from coconut husk
- Eco Coconut Dish Brush - Made from wood and coconut husk
- Eco Coconut Bottle Brush - Made from wood and coconut husk
- Wooden Pot Brush - Made from wood and plant fibres
- Washing Up Loofah - Made from Loofah plant

Washing Up Gloves

Everyone's go-to washing up gloves are the yellow Marigold gloves. These are recyclable under a Terracycle scheme but not everyone has Terracycle collections local to them

(Terracycle, 2021). To avoid plastic waste, you can get gloves made from natural rubber which are compostable at the end of their useful life. An easy swap to make as it is no change of habit.

USING A DISHWASHER

Dishwashers have a bit of a reputation for being less eco-friendly than washing up due to the fact that they use electricity and water to run. If you have a dishwasher, there are a few ways you can reduce their impact by reducing the plastic and chemicals used.

Dishwasher Tablets

There are multiple options available for dishwasher tablets that are more earth friendly. Common dishwasher tablet brands tend to contain lots of chemicals, including things like bleach which is harmful to aquatic life. You can get subscription boxes that are delivered straight to your door based on how often you use the tablets. Smol for example is a good one, that is cruelty free and is delivered in recyclable cardboard packaging. They contain less chemicals than high street brands and are concentrated to also include rinse aid and salt in one so you shouldn't need these in addition. Oxygen based bleach is used in these instead which is safe and non-toxic. Smol offer a free trial so you can try before you buy.

If you are wanting something that you can get on the high street, Wilkinson's offer eco dishwasher tablets in a cardboard box.

You can also make your own dishwasher tablets using a recipe (Kielman, n.d.). This one for example was found from a quick Google search.

Rinse Aid

If you use dishwasher tablets that don't include rinse aid, you can usually pick up rinse aid in your local refill shop. Just keep reusing the same container.

Although it's not the best alternative, you can also get Ecover rinse aid in most supermarkets.

CLEANING THE KITCHEN

Because of the kitchen's purpose, it is important to keep it clean for hygiene reasons. A lot of us therefore turn to products that contain bleach to clean our kitchens, but as mentioned above, bleach is harmful to marine life which is worrying as most of us regularly pour it down the drain.

There are a number of bleach-free kitchen cleaner sachets and anti- bacterial sachets that are plastic free and dissolve in water so that you can reuse an old bottle. Ocean Saver are one of the main brands for these. You can also get oven cleaning sachets by Iron & Velvet which follow the same concept.

If you would rather make your own kitchen cleaner, here is a recipe that you can use to make a natural alternative which I found online, although there are others available (Green and Simple, 2021):

1. Mix three parts water to one part white vinegar.
2. Add two teaspoons of bicarb soda.
3. To get rid of the vinegar smell, add a few drops of essential oils or alternatively, you can add in lemon/orange peel.

This is a great all-purpose recipe for a quick wipe down and refresh of your kitchen. If you've got stubborn stains, you'll need to spray and let the mixture soak before wiping off. PLEASE NOTE, White vinegar is not recommended for use on granite, marble, and soapstone worktops as it can cause them to lose their shine.

If you don't have an old plastic bottle to rinse out and reuse, you can get Ocean Saver recycled plastic bottles or glass ones that you can keep refilling over and over again.

LAUNDRY

Did you know that a large number of the clothes we wear are made from plastic? Acrylic jumpers and polyester shirts are some examples! These clothes when washed emit tiny plastic fibres called micro-plastics which eventually end up in our rivers and oceans. The combination of these tiny plastics and the chemicals we use to clean our clothes are contributing to the poisoning of marine life in our seas.

Although we can't eradicate these man-made fibres altogether, there are a couple of things we can do to help minimise the impact.

Laundry Detergent

There are a few alternatives to common brands of laundry detergent that are plant-based and therefore not pumping chemicals into the sea:

Laundry Sheets - **These are a plastic free alternative** that come packaged in a recyclable cardboard box, made from plant-based materials that effectively but gently clean your laundry. Transporting them emits less CO_2 as they weigh a lot less due to not containing water.

Soap Nuts - These grow on trees and use mother nature's detergent to clean your washing. A few soap nuts get put into each load of washing and can then be reused up to four times before being composted.

Refill Stores - You can usually get eco-friendly liquid laundry detergent in your local refill stores. You just need to take an old bottle to refill each time.

If you want to use a fabric softener, you can make your own using epsom salts, baking soda and essential oils. Here is an example recipe that I found (Maid Right, 2021).

1. Mix 1 cup of epsom salts and 1/4 cup of baking soda together.
2. Add 10 to 15 drops of essential oils for every full cup of epsom salts. Seal container and shake.
3. Add two to three tablespoons of this mixture directly into the washer for each load of laundry.

Some people recommend using white vinegar as a fabric softener, and although it works well, some people say that it can damage the rubber seals on washing machines so be careful when using white vinegar in your laundry.

Stain Remover

Instead of using chemicals such as Vanish in your washing to get rid of stains, you can use a natural stain remover that comes in bar form - this avoids the plastic waste and reduces the chemicals being used in your washing. You can also use Oxygen Bleach.

Preventing Micro-Plastics

The best way to prevent micro-plastics from going down the drain is to avoid clothes made with plastic materials such as polyester or nylon. That's not to say that you need to throw away all of your clothes made with these fabrics and go out and buy new. Keep wearing the same clothes until they're worn out, but when you need to replace something, it's best to opt for natural fabrics such as organic cotton, hemp and bamboo wherever possible.

In the meantime, for all of the clothes that we own that contain plastic, there are a couple of things that you can buy that can help prevent these plastics from going into the sea:

Micro Filter Wash Bags - These micro filter wash bags collect micro-plastics from your washing allowing you to dispose of them properly instead of them being washed away with the waste water. You just put all of your plastic fabrics in the bag before washing, then put the bag in the washing machine.

Cora Ball - A Cora Ball acts in the same way as a Guppy Friend wash bag, except you put the ball into the washing machine with your laundry and the micro-plastics get trapped in the ball. When the fibres build up, you can remove them with your hands and dispose of them safely.

Drying Laundry

The most eco-friendly way to dry your washing is to air dry, either indoors on an airer, or outside on a washing line. Did you know that the sun also acts as a natural stain remover and bacteria killer?

Air drying isn't always possible for some so a tumble dryer is used. These are bad for the environment as they use a lot of energy, but you can invest in dryer eggs which reduce the drying time by up to 28% and also help to naturally soften your washing. You just pop them in with your wet laundry.

KITCHEN ROLL

Research has shown that households worldwide go through 6.5 million tonnes of kitchen roll every year (Forge Recycling, 2021). To prevent this waste, you can cut up old t-shirts, pillowcases and tea towels and use these to mop up spills instead - just wash and reuse them each time.

Alternatively, if you don't have anything old to repurpose, you can buy other options. For example, Compostable Sponge Kitchen Roll.

BATHROOM

As we did with the kitchen - take a look around your bathroom and write a list of everything you see that comes in or contains plastic (some of these might surprise you!) My list is, shampoo and conditioner and other hair treatments, hair brush, hair ties, hair styling products, dry shampoo, cotton buds, shower gel and hand soap, body loofahs, bubble bath, body lotion, skin care products, make up, shaving gel and razors, dental products such as toothbrush, toothpaste, dental floss and interdental brushes, deodorant, toilet roll/wet wipes, cleaning products for the bathroom and menstrual products (I'm sure I've missed some hidden ones somewhere but this gives you an idea).

The good thing about making eco-friendly swaps is that 9 times out of 10, they include natural ingredients and don't contain nasties such as SLS and parabens which aren't very good for us. So not only are you helping the planet, but you're also taking better care of you, which is always a positive!

HAIR CARE

Shampoo and Conditioner

Have you ever used a shampoo and conditioner in the shower, dried your hair and your hair feels incredibly soft? I know I have when I used to use bottled shampoo and I always thought that meant that my hair was in great condition. The reason your hair feels amazing afterwards is most likely because it has been coated in chemicals called silicones which give you the

impression that your hair is well- nourished when in fact, it isn't. Lots of commercial brands unfortunately often include silicones in their formulas.

Luckily, there are a few alternatives that you can opt for that actually nourish your hair and are plastic free.

Shampoo Bars - These are effectively just shampoo in solid form. The majority of the time, they come packaged in cardboard boxes that can easily be recycled, and are often free from chemicals such as SLS, parabens and silicones, although not all brands are so it's worth checking the ingredients first. SLS stands for Sodium Lauryl Sulphate and silicones tend to end in -cone, -conol or -siloxane.

To use shampoo bars, it is a slightly different method to your usual liquid shampoo, but once you've done it a couple of times it will become second nature. You can either rub the bar directly on to your hair and then massage it in to create a lather (best if you have thick or long hair), or you can create a lather in your hands and apply that to your hair.

Conditioner Bars - Again, these are a solid version of bottled conditioner packaged in recyclable cardboard and they usually come in two different types. One, you use as a solid bar that you essentially just rub on the ends of your hair, and the other you melt down in boiling water to use like normal conditioner. It really just depends on your hair type and if you prefer to have a liquid to run through the ends of your hair.

2 In 1 Shampoo and Conditioner Bars - Although I found with the shampoo bars that I use, I don't need to use a conditioner (you might find the same if you try them), you can get designated 2 in 1 shampoo and conditioner bars that are designed to eliminate the need for a conditioner altogether. This is an even better option as you only need one bar instead of two.

Liquid Options in Plastic Free Packaging - If you find that you don't get on with the bars, there are liquid options you can get that are free from the chemical nasties that come in recyclable glass or aluminium packaging. You can also get powdered refills that make up a liquid shampoo.

Refill Stores - As mentioned above, most refill stores have options for shampoo and conditioner where you can take old bottles to reuse and keep refilling them. Again, these will be eco-friendly options without the chemical nasties.

Hair Brushes and Combs

I used to be guilty of going down to my local store to buy a cheap plastic hair brush that I'd use until it broke and would then chuck away. Although this is easy and budget friendly, if we add up all of the plastic hair brushes that are thrown away each year, it's a scary number!

There are a couple of options for plastic free hair brushes and combs:

Bamboo Hair Brush - Lots of bamboo hair brushes also have wooden pins instead of plastic ones so it's not just the handle that's plastic free.

Plant-Based Salon Quality Brushes - Lotus have created a salon quality detangling hair brush that is easy on your hair whilst getting rid of all of your knots. I personally use one of these. The best bit about them for me is that they are made from a plant-based material that will biodegrade when thrown away, so you're getting the best of both worlds.

Bamboo Comb - An easy plastic free alternative that is compostable at the end of its life.

HAIR TIES AND HAIR STYLING PRODUCTS

Hair ties were one of the plastic items in the bathroom that surprised me. The problem is, I'm sure I'm not the only one who takes their hair down and then cannot for love nor money find the hair tie they were using. I must have gone through countless hair ties in my lifetime, so when you think about the bigger picture, it's quite scary how many plastic hair ties are littering the planet considering they can take around 500 years to break down! Here are a few alternatives for hair ties:

Generic Hair Ties - These are made from natural rubber and organic cotton so are 100% biodegradable, sustainable and recyclable.

Organic Scrunchies - If you prefer a more stylish look and want a scrunchie, you can get these plastic free alternatives.

For hair styling, there are lots of different products so I have listed the main ones I can think of below:

Hair Gel - If you want something that will keep your hair in place, you can get hair wax and hair clays that are made from natural ingredients and come in an aluminium tin instead of plastic tub.

Due to the sticky nature of the products involved, it's unlikely that the plastic tubs containing hair gel will be recycled as they are hard to get clean.

Curly Hair Products - There are so many different types of curl products on the market, such as mousses, creams and sprays however most of these are made with chemicals and come in plastic packaging. To avoid these and use natural products, you can either choose to DIY (Shannon, 2017), or if you haven't got the time to make your own, opt for something that comes in alternative packaging, such as the Olew Curl Cream.

Hair Spray - Did you know that some of the ingredients used in conventional hair sprays are bad for our health? Also, some of the high street hair spray brands still test on animals! To avoid these, you can hold your hair in place with more environmentally friendly options, like this green tea hair spray for example, although there are other alternatives on the market.

Heat Protection - For a natural alternative to heat protection, you can use natural oils such as argan oil which is a natural heat protector (Mauldin Group, n.d.).

DRY SHAMPOO

For those that need to wash their hair regularly, swapping three showers a week to dry shampoo can save approximately 7,800 litres of water a year! It also has the added perk of adding volume to your hair in between washes.

Using a natural dry shampoo will also help with any transition phase you might experience making the swap to shampoo bars, although depending on your hair type and the shampoo bar you choose to use, not everyone will experience a transition phase. The one from KiteNest is organic, talc free, palm oil free, contains no nasties and is plastic free. You can't really go wrong with this one.

COTTON BUDS

Prior to the ban that began in October 2020, it was estimated that we used to use 1.8 billion plastic-stemmed cotton buds a year in England alone (MP, 2020). There are a few alternatives on the market that you can use in place of plastic-stemmed cotton buds:

Bamboo Cotton Buds - **These are made with bamboo, which is a fast growing plant, instead of having a plastic stem.**

Recycled Paper Cotton Buds - **Home compostable after use and completely plastic free.**

Reusable Cotton Buds - **These replace at least 1,000 disposable cotton buds. Just wash after use and keep reusing.**

SHOWER GEL AND HAND SOAP

A lot of shower gels and soap products on the market contain foaming agents such as SLS which can cause irritation, especially for those with sensitive skin or skin conditions such as Eczema or Psoriasis. They also tend to come in plastic bottles and tubs which take years to break down in landfill.

For hand soap, instead of getting your usual bottle of liquid soap to go at your kitchen and bathroom sinks, you can get natural soap bars such as the Friendly soap bars which come in cardboard packaging and contain lots of yummy natural ingredients that won't harm the environment when they go down the drain.

If you want something that will kill off germs, Tea Tree is naturally antibacterial, so the Tea Tree and Turmeric soap bar would be a good fit.

Soap bars also work well in place of shower gel, but some people don't like the squeaky feeling on their skin which can sometimes be left after use. So, if you want to use a naked alternative for shower gel, Shower Blocks have created a solid shower gel bar which contain moisturisers to prevent this squeaky feeling.

If you find that you don't get on with solid bars, you can choose to go for liquid soap and liquid shower gel which come in eco-friendly packaging. Some companies like Beauty Kitchen offer return schemes for their metal bottles so that they can be refilled and reused to prevent waste.

BATHROOM ACCESSORIES

Soap Dishes

If you have made the swap to solid soap bars, you will need somewhere to store them on the side of the sink to help prolong their life and keep the bacteria at bay. Some free hacks to do this are:

- Stick a beer bottle lid into the soap bar to rest the soap on when it's on the side of the sink. This prevents the bar from sitting in water as it is slightly raised.
- Repurpose an old food carton or yoghurt pot

If you want something that is aesthetically pleasing, you can get natural soap rests made of compostable fibres, or soap dishes made from bamboo, wood or ceramics. Just make sure that there is somewhere for the water to drain to stop the bar from sitting in water.

Body Loofahs and Sponges

The first thing that comes to mind when I think of a sponge or a loofah is the round sponges from the supermarket that I used to use when I was a kid, and the brightly coloured plastic loofahs that come in a beauty gift set. The good news though is that there are alternatives for these if you like to use something alongside your shower gel or soap in the shower.

Tabitha Eve Bath Sponge - Made with soft cotton and gentle bamboo which is naturally antibacterial. Brilliant for the bathroom and gentle for baby.

Body Konjac Sponge - Made with sustainable plant roots for gentle everyday exfoliation.

Body Loofah - Great for a natural way to exfoliate. Made from the loofah plant. These feel quite dry and stiff when they are dry, but they expand and soften when they are wet.

BATH PRODUCTS

Bubble bath, although not a necessity, is a nice luxury to have when you want to unwind after a long day. There are a few natural plastic free options that you can use instead of plastic bath products that contain foaming agents such as SLS.

Bubble Bars - These are solid bars that you break off and crumble into the bath to create the bubbles. Beauty Kubes make a couple of options, and Rowdy Kind make one that is suitable for children over the age of 3.

Bath Salts - Bath salts are great for soaking your aching muscles. Luckily, it's quite easy these days to find plastic free, vegan and cruelty free bath salts so there are lots of different options available.

BODY LOTIONS

Our skin comes into contact with so many elements every day, so it's a good idea to look after it and restore it regularly. Unfortunately, a large number of commercial brands include silicones and other plastics in their body lotions. Not only this, but they are also packaged in plastic tubs; sometimes with a box and plastic wrap round the outside too - all of which is unnecessary.

There are a couple of options that you can turn to for body lotions that are packed with natural skin loving ingredients, such as liquid body lotions that come in an aluminium tin, or solid lotion bars that come in bar form in a recyclable cardboard box.

SKIN CARE PRODUCTS

Did you know that our skin absorbs whatever we put on it? I don't know about you, but that motivates me to cut out all of the toxins and only use natural skin loving products.

Most skin care products on the high street come in plastic tubs and tubes. Although these are made from recyclable plastic, they need to be thoroughly cleaned beforehand which means that they probably aren't actually recycled due to the nature of the products inside (you'll know what I mean if you've ever tried to wash out a pot of moisturiser!)

Below is a list of some products that I would recommend for your face skin care routine that come in plastic free packaging and are free from nasties. I have personally used most of these and love what they do. The ones I haven't used myself I have quoted as I have heard brilliant reviews for them.

Cleansers

- **UpCircle Face Cleansing Balm** - Made from repurposed apricot stones from the apricot industry which would have otherwise ended up in landfill
- **Friendly Face Cleansing Soap Bar** - Great for those with sensitive skin as it only contains a few ingredients, all natural of course.
- **Lani Blue Mint Cleanser** - Powder cleanser that you add water to, to create a paste. Easier to prevent waste with a powder than a liquid.

Toners

- **Flawless Hydrating Toner** - Packaged in a glass bottle with an aluminium lid and free from all nasties.
- **UpCircle Face Toner** - Made with repurposed chamomile stem extract (a by-product of the tea industry) and repurposed residual water of green mandarin fruit (a by-product of the juicing industry).

Moisturisers

- **UpCircle Face Moisturiser** - Made with repurposed finely-ground powder of discarded argan shells, a natural by-product of the argan oil industry that otherwise would have ended up in landfill.
- **Purity Youth Glow Face Cream** - Packaging comes with a paper casing that contains seeds to plant in your garden.

Eye Creams

- UpCircle Eye Cream - Made with coffee oil extracted from repurposed grounds and anti-inflammatory maple bark extract, a by-product of the wood industry.

- Purity Natural Beauty Radiance Eye Gel - Packaging comes with a paper casing that contains seeds to plant in your garden.

Face Serums

- Lani Tropical Super Serum - A great all-rounder. Available with a pipette and with an aluminium lid to 'refill' when you run out.

- Lani Tropical Night Serum - A light serum to give your skin all the nutrients it needs to restore overnight. Available with a pipette and with an aluminium lid to 'refill' when you run out.

- Lani Omega Glow Serum - Full of skin loving ingredients to start the day. Available with a pipette and with an aluminium lid to 'refill' when you run out.

Face Scrubs

- UpCircle Coffee Scrub - Made with coffee grounds from cafes around London that would otherwise have ended up in landfill. Available in three variants to suit different skin types.

- Make your own! There are lots of different recipes online, but this is a relatively easy blackhead busting one that I found online, which is made with things that are likely to already be in your cupboard (Price, 2020):

Ingredients:

- ½ tsp lemon
- 1 tbsp salt
- 1 tsp purified/distilled water

1. Mix it all together and rub the paste onto skin in a circular motion.
2. Gently scrub for two to three minutes, being careful not to rub too hard.
3. Rinse off with warm water and follow with the rest of your skincare routine.

Face Masks

- Lani Tropical Cacao Detox Mask - Packaged in a glass jar with an aluminium lid.
- UpCircle Face Mask - Made with the finely-ground powder of discarded olive stones, a natural by-product of the olive oil industry and a powerful anti-inflammatory.
- Make your own! Again, there are lots of different recipes online, but this is another one I found that is likely to include things already in your cupboard (Elezovic, 2020). For tired looking skin - just mix it all together and apply to your skin.

Ingredients:

- Juice of 1 lemon
- 2 tablespoons sugar
- 1 tablespoon olive oil

UpCircle (UpCircle, 2021) have provided a guide on their recommended skin care routine. I previously wrote a blog post on this which you can find on my website if you are looking for guidance on which order to use your products and how often.

Cotton Wool Alternatives

If you cleanse and tone your face twice a day as recommended, you are most likely using between 730 and 1,460 cotton wool pads - not including any pads used for removing eye make-up etc. Shop bought cotton wool is single-use and isn't very environmentally friendly to produce. So, it's always better to switch to a reusable alternative. I have included some alternatives that you can purchase below:

- Reusable cotton wool pads
- Muslin cloths
- Bamboo face cloths

If you want a tip for free alternatives, you can always cut up an old t-shirt or tea towel, or just use a flannel.

Make-Up

Make-up products are one of the harder areas to completely eradicate plastic and toxins, but after some research, I have found a couple of different brands and products that tick most boxes.

Unfortunately, I don't think the perfect products exist yet due to their nature. For example, with mascara, it's inevitable that there will be an element of plastic for the mascara wand etc.

Refillable Make-Up Products

The best all-round brand that I have found so far for make-up is Zao. Most of their products come packaged in a bamboo outer with refillable options, so you purchase the whole product  initially and then only need to buy the refill when it runs out. This includes everything from foundation, mascara, eye shadow, bronzer and even lipstick and lip gloss.

You can find the whole range from Zao on their website.

If you like a mineral foundation, I personally found All Earth mineral cosmetics to be fantastic. They also use bamboo packaging that you can refill when you run out.

Other Brands

For mascara, if you want to avoid plastic altogether, I have come across a mascara cake which comes in a metal tin. To apply it, you can use an old mascara wand.

TOP TIP - As mascara wands are pretty much unavoidable if you wear mascara, there is a great way that they can be repurposed. Mascara wands are perfect for combing the fur and feathers of small wildlife to remove fleas, larva and fly eggs. So before chucking away your old mascara wands, wash them out and get in contact with local animal charities to see if you can donate them. If you don't have a local centre, you can post off your mascara wands to Appalachian Wildlife Refuge directly using the form on their website (Appalachain Wild, n.d.).

RAZORS AND SHAVING

Most mainstream razors last anywhere between 3 and 10 uses before they start to work less efficiently (Gillette Venus, 2021). If you're a regular shaver, this adds up to a large amount of waste ending up in landfill. Although Gillette have partnered up with Terracycle, which is a step in the right direction, unfortunately the collection points available aren't always accessible to everyone. But fear not! There are plastic free alternatives available.

Safety Razors

If you've ever seen a safety razor, you'll know they look a bit like a medieval weapon, but don't let that put you off! Most people who have made the switch (including myself) say that it is the smoothest and closest shave they've ever had! Although there is a slight change in technique, they're essentially exactly the same as a disposable razor for both men and women. The main differences are that you go with the grain of the hair instead of against it (down your leg instead of up it for example) and that you don't apply any pressure; just glide it along.

The one I use is the Edwin Jagger DE Safety Razor but there are plenty of options available on the market. All you have to replace with a safety razor is the blades. You can save up your used blades in a blade bank to keep them safely stored, and then when the bank is full you can recycle the blades and the bank together.

Shaving Soap

Did you know that some shaving foams/creams include a form of plastic in the ingredients? Examples include PEG products and Glyceryl Acrylate - check your shaving foam cans to see if they include these ingredients.

A shaving soap is a solid alternative to shaving cream or gel. The only difference is that you create a lather and use that to shave with instead of using foam. The best one I have come across is the Friendly shaving soap which is completely vegan, cruelty free, plastic free and palm oil free.

Dental

Taking care of our teeth is important, not just for our health but for our own personal confidence. If you ask most people what they notice first about a person, it is their smile. The good news is that it is possible to take care of your teeth whilst also taking care of the planet by removing the chemicals and plastic packaging.

Toothbrushes

The first eco-friendly alternative most people turn to is the bamboo toothbrush. Although the bristles tend to be made from a type of Nylon which is plastic, these can be removed, and the handle will biodegrade so there is a lot less plastic waste going to landfill than with a conventional plastic toothbrush.

As the handle is made from bamboo, some people can experience mould growing on the end of the handle if it has been sat in water. To combat this, Barnaby's Brushes created a bamboo toothbrush that has a stainless-steel handle which will last a lifetime - you just have to replace the bamboo head each time which in my opinion is a better alternative as there is even less waste being produced.

If you prefer to use an electric toothbrush, you can swap your plastic toothbrush heads for ones that can be recycled by the manufacturer. These are available for Oral-B toothbrushes and Philips Sonicare toothbrushes.

Interdental Brushes - Lots of dentists recommend the use of interdental brushes to prevent gum disease by getting rid of food and plaque from between your teeth. Most of these are made from plastic, but you can opt for bamboo ones that you can compost after use.

Dental Floss

31% of Brits clean between their teeth each day (Smith, 2017) and as most conventional flosses aren't recyclable or plastic-free, a lot of the dental floss used in the UK ends up in landfill or being incinerated. To prevent this waste, you don't have to avoid flossing.

You can opt for a refillable and compostable dental floss which is plastic free and can be put in the compost bin after use.

Toothpaste Alternatives

Around 300 million empty toothpaste tubes are sent to landfill every year (Hall, 2021). If that isn't scary enough, did you know that toothpaste itself can actually contain plastic? Check your toothpaste tube and see if any of the ingredients start with 'poly'. This unfortunately means that every time we clean our teeth, we are potentially sending microplastics into the environment whilst also potentially consuming some ourselves!

There are a few different alternatives for toothpaste which you can choose instead of the usual toothpaste we see on the shelves:

Toothpaste Tablets - These are a toothpaste that come in tablet form. You chew the tablet to trigger the foaming and then brush like normal.

Natural Toothpaste - Georganics is a brand that have created a natural, organic, cruelty free and plastic free toothpaste that comes in a glass jar with an aluminium lid. You use it the same as normal toothpaste except instead of squeezing it out of a tube, you scoop it out of a jar. This brand doesn't contain Fluoride but the Ben & Anna one does if you would prefer to use Fluoride.

Georganics also make a tooth soap and a toothpaste powder if you want to try something completely different to the norm.

You can also make your own toothpaste using the recipe below which I found from a quick search (Wells, 2021), although please note that this doesn't contain fluoride (other recipes available):

Ingredients:
- ½ cup coconut oil.
- 2-3 TBSP baking soda.
- 2 small packets stevia powder.
- 15-20 drops peppermint essential oil

1. Melt/soften the coconut oil.
2. Mix in other ingredients and stir.
3. Pour the mixture into a small glass jar.
4. Let cool completely.

If you want to stick to the high street brands we all know, Colgate recently created a more eco-friendly toothpaste called 'Smile For Good' which comes in a recyclable tube and carton, and is vegan. This is a great step in the right direction, and I hope the other big brands will follow suit. I have seen this toothpaste available in most supermarkets and places like Wilkinson's and have tried it myself.

Mouthwash

Although some don't consider mouthwash a necessity, others have been advised to use it or like to use it to feel fresh. High street mouthwashes contain lots of chemicals to 'work wonders' on your teeth - to get rid of bad breath, or whiten teeth etc. They also come in plastic bottles.

To avoid the chemicals and plastic, you can either choose to use an alternative such as mouthwash tablets which you dissolve in water before using as normal mouthwash or opt for the ancient technique of oil pulling. This is where you swish oil around your mouth for a period of time (usually around 20 minutes) to remove toxins and improve your oral health. You can use coconut oil and olive oil or can purchase a ready-made oil from somewhere like Georganics.

Chewing Gum

Chewing gum contains hidden plastics which means that we are literally chewing on plastic. It also means that all of the gum we see stuck to the pavement are small pieces of plastic pollution. Luckily, you don't have to forgo this little pleasure!

There are plastic free alternatives that still give you the same experience.

NATURAL DEODORANTS

Most high street deodorants contain aluminium which is designed to block your pores and stop you sweating (anti-perspirants). Natural deodorants are formulated to still allow you to sweat but neutralise any odour without stopping your body from doing what it was designed to do. We have been programmed to think that sweating is bad, but in fact it is a healthy bodily function.

There are a number of different alternatives on the market including roll-ons that come in a cardboard tube, and ones you apply with your fingers that are packaged in a glass jar.

Most natural deodorants contain sodium bicarbonate although each brand use different quantities. If you have sensitive skin, you may find that you will need to use a bicarb-free deodorant as sodium bicarbonate can sometimes cause skin irritation.

If you have sensitive skin, then I would recommend The Natural Deodorant Co Gentle Range which are free from sodium bicarbonate. Both alternatives including the Gentle Range can be found on the Resource Page.

TOILET PAPER

Although toilet roll is not made of plastic, it still has quite a poor environmental footprint. According to National Geographic, toilet paper wipes out 27,000 trees a day (Braun, 2010) which is depleting the world's forests. Most toilet paper brands in the supermarket are packaged in plastic which also adds to the plastic problem.

Some supermarkets have started to produce toilet paper that comes in recyclable paper packaging which is a step in the right direction, and some have also started producing toilet rolls made from recycled paper.

If your local supermarket doesn't stock these alternatives, there are a number of online brands that sell bulk boxes of toilet rolls that come with no packaging. Some are made of bamboo, which is a lot faster growing that regular trees, or made from recycled paper.

Here are a few below but there are lots of options available if you search online.

Who Gives A Crap - **Bamboo**
Serious Tissues - **Recycled paper**

Uranus Wiper - Recycled paper
Naked Sprout - Unbleached bamboo

WET WIPES

Most wet wipes are made primarily of plastic which is really quite upsetting given that they were designed to be flushed down the toilet. They cause fatbergs in sewers which adds to the microplastic pollution in the ocean and are also the third most common litter item found on UK beaches. See more information in the article linked on the Resource Page (BBC, 2021).

The best thing to do for the environment is to avoid wipes altogether, but if you must use wipes, you can get plastic free wet wipes online and, in some supermarkets, or can get reusable wipes from somewhere like Cheeky Wipes.

CLEANING THE BATHROOM

Again, this is an important area of the house to clean regularly. Most of us tend to use things like bleach to clean the toilet and keep your ceramics gleaming white. But there is another way to thoroughly clean your bathroom that doesn't require harsh chemicals like this.

There are a number of bathroom cleaner sachets that are plastic free and dissolve in water so that you can reuse an old bottle. Ocean Saver are one of the main brands for these.

Toilet Cleaning

Unfortunately, wipes are the go-to product to clean the toilet seat these days. As mentioned above, wipes are awful for the environment, so these are best avoided.

I personally use a bamboo cloth (that I wash after each use) along with the Ocean Saver antibacterial cleaner to clean the toilet seat. To make sure I use the same cloth each time, I have a different colour for each thing, so for instance I know the blue one is for the loo and the pink one is for the sink (the rhyming helps me to remember which is which).

If you feel the need to use disposable wipes, then I know that Wilkinson's do plastic free antibacterial wipes that you can use instead, although I would suggest that these are a last resort. Wilkinson's is where I have seen these alternatives, but please note that there may also be ones available elsewhere as well.

Instead of using bleach down the bowl of the toilet, you can purchase or make your own toilet cleaning bombs. These are a concoction of natural ingredients which you put down the toilet bowl. For more information on these ingredients, see the 'Cleaning' section further on in the book.

To make your own, here is an example recipe that I have personally used in the past, but there are others available:

Ingredients:
- 1 cup baking soda

- 1/4 cup citric acid
- 20 drops essential oil of your choice (I used Tea Tree)
- 1 table spoon of Castille soap or washing up liquid
- Silicone ice cube mould

1. Add all of the ingredients together into a bowl and mix together by hand until the mixture resembles wet sand.
2. Put into the silicone mould and leave to set for a couple of hours.

MENSTRUAL PRODUCTS

Over a lifetime, a single woman will use more than 11,000 disposable menstrual products (Hampson, 2019), most of which are made of plastic. It has also been found that these disposable sanitary products contain some nasty toxic substances which can affect our health. If that isn't scary enough, some other scary facts about menstrual products can be found at Wen (Wen, n.d.) - Wen Environmenstrual fact sheet.

To prevent the above, there are a couple of options available:

Menstrual Cup - This is a small funnel shaped cup made of silicone or rubber that you insert like a tampon. They don't need changing as regularly (you can wear them for up to 12 hours), and after washing, it can be reused instead of throwing it away. I know this doesn't sound appealing, but it's not anywhere near as bad as you think it's going to be. I've used one in the past and once you get the hang of it, they are an amazing alternative.

There are lots of brands available on the market which can make it quite overwhelming knowing which one to choose. Luckily, there is a quiz you can take called 'Put A Cup In It' which will help you find the best fit for you.

Reusable Sanitary Products - These are a good alternative if you don't like the idea of using a cup or want something that is like the norm. These are essentially just sanitary towels and pantyliners that are made from materials like bamboo and cotton, but instead of throwing them away afterwards, you pop them in the wash and reuse. If looked after properly, they should last years. Lots of small businesses hand make them. You can usually find these by searching on social media. Alternatively, there are bigger companies that make them such as Cheeky Wipes.

Cheeky Wipes (and other companies) also offer period pants, which are just usual pants with a pad essentially build in. These are great if you want to feel like you're not wearing anything! I use these and recommend them.

You can also get disposable brands that are free of plastic and free from the chemical nasties for those that don't like the reusable concept for sanitary products. Yoppie and TOTM are some examples.

OUT & ABOUT

When we are out and about, it is very easy to choose convenience over sustainability. For example, getting a plastic take-away cup from the coffee shop because we don't have time to sit in, or grabbing a bottle of water from the shop to quench our thirst. With a bit of pre-planning, it's easy to make changes to avoid plastic when out for the day. Take a look at the suggestions below:

FOOD AND DRINK

Reusable Bottles

Instead of grabbing a single use plastic bottle to keep you hydrated whilst you're out and about, fill up a reusable bottle before you go with the beverage of your choice and take that with you. That way, you are avoiding the single use plastic bottle.

According to Recycle Now, it is estimated that an average o 35.8 million plastic bottles are used every day in the UK, but only 19.8 million are recycled each day. This means there are on average 16 million plastic bottles a day not making their way into the recycling bin and ending up in landfill or polluting the environment (Recycle Now, n.d.). This is one of those times that I think the quote "it's just one water bottle, said 35.8 million people" helps to put things into perspective!

There are a few different options available:

- Glass Bottle - These are great for any cold drinks like water, juice and iced tea or coffee, however, aren't the best choice for clumsy people.

- If this is you, then you can get a stainless-steel one - also great for kids! These are a good option for keeping your drinks hot or cold, depending which you choose to use it for as most are insulated.

Reusable Coffee Cups

Lots of coffee shops are starting to realise the impact their disposable coffee cups are having on the planet and are now starting to opt for recyclable or compostable cups, which is a great step in the right direction. However, these are still single use items so why not take your own coffee cup to reuse instead?

An added perk to this is that lots of coffee shops are now giving monetary incentives for using a reusable cup, by

...ou a small discount. For example, Costa offer a 25p someone using a reusable cup.

This doesn't sound a lot, but if you got a cup of coffee to go 5 days a week for a year, that is a whopping £65 discount for enjoying the same cup of coffee, just packaged slightly differently.

Again, here are a few different options that you can choose:

- Insulated coffee cup
- Glass coffee cup
- Collapsible coffee cup

Lunch and Take-aways

When taking food out, it's easy to hunt out the cling film or the tinned foil to wrap your lunch and snacks in. Cling film is the definition of single-use plastic, so it is best to avoid this altogether.

If you want an alternative to wrap food in instead of cling film or foil, you can use reusables such as beeswax wraps, reusable sandwich wraps or silicone food pouches to wrap your food in. Links to these are listed on the Eco-Sal Resource Page.

For taking snacks or lunch, my first port of call is to reuse old takeaway containers. If you don't have a stash of these, or something already at home that you can reuse, there are plastic free lunch boxes that you can get. Although plastic lunch boxes are not single use plastics, it's still better to avoid plastic if you can so that when they come to the end of their life, they won't be cluttering up landfills for hundreds of years.

Some options for plastic free lunchboxes include:
- Huski Home Rice Husk Lunch
- Elephant Box Metal Lunch Box

If you are wanting a take away meal one night, it's quite difficult these days to find takeaways that don't use the plastic tubs. The best thing to do here is speak to your local takeaways to see if they allow you to bring your own containers when you go to collect. If they don't, you can always reuse the plastic tubs as lunch boxes or for storing food in the fridge. Alternatively, some homeless shelters take the plastic pots to reuse giving food to the homeless so it's worth checking with any local shelters to see if they accept them.

Straws

Although straws aren't considered a necessity to most, some simply like to use them, and some have to use them for medical purposes. In this scenario, you can get reusable straws such as metal and bamboo straws which you can clean and keep reusing. As they're small, they can easily fit into things like your handbag to carry around with you. You can also keep them in the car if you end up having fast food - just refuse the straw when you order. Although lots of fast food chains have switched from plastic straws to paper straws, they are still not actually recyclable as their thickness makes them difficult to process.

Carrier Bags

We've all been a culprit of forgetting our carrier bags when we go to the supermarket or out shopping for the day and having to get the 5p plastic ones. Even if we do already have a massive stash of them sat in the car. My tip here is to always have a couple folded up in your handbag/coat pocket or in the front seat of your car for those unexpected trips to the shops and keep a load together in the boot that you can easily access when you go food shopping.

When the plastic ones come to break, instead of buying more from the supermarkets, try to get hard wearing ones made from natural fibres like jute. These will last a lot longer so will avoid waste, and as they are natural fibres, they avoid creating more plastic waste later on.

SUN CREAM

Sun cream is an important essential for us to look after our skin and prevent sun damage that can cause cancer. A lot of the high street brands, however come packaged in plastic bottles, and contain a large number of unpronounceable chemicals. Holiday makers who swim in the sea are contributing to coral bleaching as some of these chemicals in their sun cream seep into the water and are absorbed by the corals.

There are a couple of brands of sun cream that you can get that come packaged in aluminium and don't contain these harsh chemicals. This is not an exhaustive list.

- Shade Suncream - This brand only contains four natural ingredients which gives effective protection against UVA and UVB rays.

- Amazinc Suncream - This brand offers a number of different alternative sun creams and oils.

PLASTERS AND MEDICINES

Most high street plasters are made of plastic so won't biodegrade in landfill. Patch plasters are made with bamboo fibres that completely biodegrade in 6 weeks in your home compost.

Unfortunately, pill packets are necessary and aren't currently recycled kerbside, but are being collected by most Superdrug stores for recycling (Briggs, 2021). You can check on their website to see if your local store is accepting them.

PARENTING

PREPARING FOR YOUR LITTLE ONE

Having a baby is such a special time. Your loved ones are filled with excitement and want to shower you with gifts for your new arrival, which is a wonderful gesture. But for those of us that want to reduce waste, it's hard to know how to handle it without sounding ungrateful to those dearest to you.

Gifts and Baby Showers

The first thing to remember is that your friends and family know you. They won't be surprised when you ask them to be sustainable with their gifting. If you are having a baby shower, don't feel awkward asking your baby shower planner to remind your guests of your ecological ethics.

My sister planned my baby shower for me and when she first started preparations, she told everyone that I was not expecting gifts at all but suggested that if people wanted to get us something, would they mind looking for:

- Their favourite childhood book which they can write a message in instead of buying a card. That way it could be kept and used.

- Clothes made from 100% organic cotton (most shops do this nowadays for baby clothes)

- Plastic free or good condition pre-owned toys and baby gyms wherever possible.

The person who plans your baby shower is normally someone close to you (mum, sister, best friend) so it should be quite easy to tell them what you want and don't want without feeling bad.

With baby showers, it's easy to get swept up in all of the decorations and games. My tips here would be to arrange games that don't come with a lot of waste (i.e. the 'smell the nappy' game involves wasting nappies and food so try to avoid games like this) and avoid balloon arches unless they are made from natural latex.

My sister and mum came up with the idea of setting up a baby washing line as a decoration, which had baby things hanging from it which we would actually use when the baby arrived. That way it wasn't wasteful. This is just one idea but there are lots of other things. Pinterest is a great place to get ideas.

Baby Goodies

When getting the final bits and bobs together in readiness for your little one's arrival, it is inevitable that some things will have to be plastic. For example, baby medicines like Calpol, and creams to help adjust to breastfeeding, are all likely to come packaged in plastic tubes and tubs. There are very few alternatives to this so just try to wash out and recycle what you can.

With your first child, it's very easy to get carried away with all of the things people and books tell you are 'essentials'. The simple fact is, a lot of these things are gimmicks and you don't actually need as much as you think you do. Avoid falling for marketing tactics and buying excessive amounts of baby products. One of the things we found on an essentials list before our little boy was born, was a teddy that plays white noise (Ewan The Sheep) which automatically plays white noise when baby is unsettled. We got one of these initially and then found that he didn't like it and preferred to just listen to womb noises on Spotify or YouTube. So, in the end we sent the teddy back and used the downloaded womb noises track from Spotify through a speaker when he slept.

For play mats, jumperoos, toys, travel cots and baby baths (and much more) you can usually find lots of these pre-owned on places like Facebook Marketplace in your area. You can pick and choose ones that are in good condition and after a clean down and maybe a wash in the machine (depending what it is), it will be good as new! These things are usually only in use for a few months before being cast aside, so it's better to get the use out of them by giving it a second, third and fourth life with a different child before it comes to the end of its useful life and is thrown away.

The same can be said for clothes. If you have a family member or friend who has had a little one of the same gender as your new arrival, you can ask them if you can have their hand-me-downs so that they get a second life. I know that there is a stigma with second-hand items, but there should be no shame in this. We should feel more embarrassed by unnecessary waste. When you're then finished with your second-hand items, if you don't have anyone to pass them on to, you can always give them to charity shops/car boot sales/put them for sale online so that other people can get some more use out of them.

NAPPIES AND WET WIPES

Nappies and wet wipes are of course, essential with a new-born. Unfortunately, most high street brands for these things are made of plastic. An average child will use 7,000 nappies until they are potty trained (Miller-Wilson, 2021), and around 12,000 wet wipes in a year (Dixon, n.d.)! These are crazy numbers when you consider how much plastic is contained in these products and this is for just one child. A little-known fact is that most wet wipes are made with 90% plastic (Sutton, 2019). If you want to avoid the throwaway nature of these items, you can opt for reusables.

Nappies

When I was pregnant with my little one, I said to a few people that I was going to use reusables and I got a few turned up noses and comments about it. But I don't understand what the stigma is with them; after all, what did people use before we had disposables? Disposables aren't always what they're cracked up to be.

There are lots of positives to using cloth nappies that you wouldn't necessarily think of (not including the obvious benefits to the environment):

- They're more reliable than disposables - Lots of cloth nappies come with two pieces, which makes them better at containing explosive poos.

- Cost - Although there is an initial outlay for cloth nappies, they can be used until your little one is toilet trained and can also be reused for any further children you have so the cost savings long term are worth it.

- On average, children in cloth nappies toilet train approximately six months earlier than their peers in disposables as they can feel when they are wet and therefore make an earlier connection between bladder release and a wet nappy. Obviously, this is child-dependant (The Nappy Lady, n.d.).

There are lots of different brands for cloth nappies that you can choose from and it can be a bit overwhelming knowing which ones to get, especially as it is quite a large financial outlay. The Nappy Lady has an online questionnaire which

helps to narrow down which brand will suit you best.
If you would prefer the disposable option, there are a few different brands which offer plastic free nappies. Some of these are also available at supermarkets:

- Eco By Naty
- Kit & Kin
- Mum & You

Wet Wipes

Not only are reusable wet wipes better for the environment, but they are also better for your baby's skin. They're usually very soft and protect your baby's skin from the harmful chemicals and scents contained in lots of disposable baby wipes. Cheeky Wipes offer lots of different kits that start at just the wipes, to including all the storage pots and essential oils. They work the same as any disposable wipe, except you wash them after use instead of throwing them away. I use these and I love them - wouldn't use anything else now.

Again, if you would prefer the disposable option for wet wipes, the above companies also do plastic free wet wipes.

BABY BOTTLES AND DUMMIES

It goes without saying that the most ecological way to feed a baby is breast feeding. Not all women can or want to do this though and therefore choose to bottle feed.

Most common brands of baby bottle like Tommee Tippee are made from plastic and have silicone teats. Although these aren't single use, it is better for the environment to avoid plastic bottles if possible and to opt for glass bottles with natural rubber teats. This way, the materials that make up the bottle are not man-made and therefore will biodegrade when the bottles are eventually thrown away.

Glass bottle brands:

- Hevea
- Kidly
- Mam

Dummies

Pretty much all dummies you see in the shops are made of plastic. Some parents try not to use dummies from birth, but if you choose to use them, you can get dummies made from natural rubber rather than silicone or latex which will biodegrade after use.

BABY FOOD

With a young one, it's really easy to opt for convenience including buying readymade baby food, some of which come in plastic pouches. There is absolutely nothing wrong with this, but if you are wanting to reduce your waste, here are a few tips:

- If you want to get readymade baby food, choose the brands that are packaged in glass jars instead of pouches wherever possible.

- If you do opt for the pouches, Terracycle recycle baby food pouches.

- When you can, try to give them the food you eat instead of pre- packed meals.

- When they're older, you can make your own ice lollies and snacks with them as an activity.

CLEANING

Advertisers have convinced us that cleaning has to involve chemical products in order for things to be 'clean'. This is not the case at all. There are a number of natural cleaners that do just as good a job. I have gone through some of these below:

NATURAL CLEANING PRODUCTS

Baking Soda

This can be found in most supermarkets in the baking section, but if you want one that comes in a cardboard box, Wilkinson's do this. You can also get some in compostable packaging.

Baking soda can be used for:

- Removing foul-smells from your fridge. Wipe the fridge shelves down with a damp cloth sprinkled with baking soda.

- It is a great cleaner for kitchen worktops, stainless steel sinks, microwaves, cooker hoods and cooking utensils. To clean your stainless-steel sink, make a paste of baking soda and white vinegar. Soak a sponge in the solution and wipe down the sink.

- Deodorise your upholstery and carpets - just sprinkle it on, leave it for 15 minutes and hoover up.

- Get rid of soap scum from your bathroom - sprinkle some baking soda on a damp cloth and rub on sinks and bathtubs to remove stubborn soap scum.

- To stop your bin from smelling - Sprinkle some baking soda in to the bottom of your bin once a week (Meredith, 2019).

White Vinegar

White vinegar is a great natural cleaner due to its acidity, however there are a couple of areas that you need to be careful with when using white vinegar.

You should NEVER use white vinegar to clean the following:

- Granite, marble, and soapstone kitchen worktops: Acids don't mix with natural stones like these.

- Egg-based messes: Vinegar will cause the proteins in the egg to coagulate, creating a gluey substance that is difficult to clean up.

- Solid wood and metal surfaces - The vinegar can remove the finishes on these materials (Nystul, 2020).

It is, however, a great cleaner for the following and there are lots more recipes and ideas that can be easily found from a quick search online.

- To give your dishwasher a clean - You don't need to buy one of these one-time dishwasher cleaners that come in a plastic bottle. Just fill a bowl with white vinegar and put it on the top shelf of the dishwasher. Then run a complete wash cycle on the hottest setting.

- To unclog a drain - Pour a half cup of baking soda and a half cup white vinegar down the drain. Cover the drain and let the mixture do its thing for a few minutes. Pour a pot of boiling water down the drain. The baking soda and vinegar dissolve any fats that are stuck in the drain.

- To get rid of hard water deposits around taps and on your shower head - For taps, soak a cloth or piece of material in white vinegar and wrap it around the area affected. Leave for an hour or more. For shower heads, remove the shower head from the hose and put it in a bucket. Cover the shower head in white vinegar and leave for an hour. Rinse it off (Nystul, 2020).

- To remove hard water stains in the toilet bowl. Just pour it down the toilet and leave overnight.

Lemon

The acidity of lemons makes it a great cleaner, like white vinegar and it also has antiseptic and antibacterial properties. There are lots of different ways you can use lemons in your cleaning regime, but here are a couple of examples.

- To clean mirrors and glass - If you don't like the smell of vinegar, squeeze 3 tablespoons of lemon juice into a spray bottle and add a cup of water. Shake and use straight away.

- To clean metal taps and plugs - Apply half a lemon directly to the tap and plug. Wipe off and buff.

- To descale the kettle - Mix 1 ounce of lemon juice to 2 cups of water and pour it into your kettle. Boil it and then let cool. Empty the kettle and give it a good rinse.

Citric Acid

Citric acid kills bacteria, mould, and mildew and is great at removing soap scum, hard water stains, calcium deposits and rust.

As it is naturally occurring, it will biodegrade naturally after use.

Many of the uses for citric acid have already been mentioned above with the other natural cleaning options, so you could substitute citric acid for most of these.

Mixtures of the above substances can be used to make things like a multi-purpose cleaner and toilet bombs. You can get citric acid in a cardboard box in Wilkinson's or in compostable packaging.

If you prefer to use ready-made products instead of making your own, there are a few options available including plant based cleaning pods which dissolve in water, and multi-purpose cleaning sheets which you can use for everything from washing up liquid to dishwasher tablets to a cleaning agent for your home. See these cleaning products on the Resource Page.

SPONGES AND CLOTHS

Did you know that most common kitchen sponges and cloths are made from plastic and can't be recycled or composted? Some of them actually send micro-plastics down the drain when they're in use!

To clean your home, you don't need to use the little green and yellow scratchy sponges and microfibre cloths. There are a few really good alternatives available:

- Compostable cleaning sponges - These are made from cellulose which is a wood fibre and make great cleaning sponges, particularly for the kitchen and bathroom. Not only are they compostable, but you can clean and disinfect them which greatly prolongs their useful life.

- Compostable sponge cloths - These are made from 70% cellulose and 30% cotton and I find are perfect for cleaning the sink, kitchen worktops, cupboards, and floors.

- Bamboo dish cloth - Made from organic bamboo, these are naturally antibacterial so make great kitchen dish cloths as they don't smell. As they come in a variety of colours, I find this helpful as I can colour code them for different cleaning functions. For example, blue is for the loo, and pink is for the sink (as said earlier in the book, the rhyming helps me to remember - it might help you too!).

OTHER CHANGES

Unfortunately, plastic pollution is not the only threat currently facing the planet. There are a number of other problems that need addressing, such as carbon emissions, water usage, and the vulnerability of nature (deforestation and species becoming endangered/extinct). I have gone through the main sections below to give some general tips and tricks on ways that you can help reduce your impact.

The horrible truth is that we are crazily overpopulated, and our natural resources like water if not used sustainably will soon not be enough to cater for the world's population. It is therefore important to save our natural resources wherever we can and not waste.

Carbon Emissions

- First things first, the easiest change you make here is to switch energy provider. Although most energy companies are now starting to offer renewable options, not all do and therefore it's best to make the switch to one that is solely renewable. The two most popular currently are Bulb and Octopus (we personally use Octopus and don't have any complaints). Both of these offer incentives to sign up if you know an existing customer who can refer you (if you get someone to sign you up, both parties get £50 credit), so it's worth seeing if any of your friends and family are with these providers before switching.

Following on from this, swap your light bulbs (when they run out) to energy saving light bulbs like LEDs, and turn off appliances and lights after use. Even the standby light on appliances uses a surprising amount of energy a year.

- To state the obvious, another way you can easily reduce your carbon footprint is to walk, cycle or car share/take public transport over driving. Not only is walking or cycling a good way to reduce emissions, but it is also better for your health and mental wellbeing. Win win!

- Get a smart meter fitted. Although these don't directly reduce carbon emissions, they help you to see how much energy you are using so that you can be more aware and monitor your usage.

For the more expensive options:

- Invest in a hybrid/electric car. You will need to charge these with electricity, but you will be reducing your carbon footprint every time you drive, plus saving money on fuel bills.

- Invest in solar panels for your house. Although there is an initial outlay, you can be sure that your energy is coming from renewable sources and also, might get some money back from energy companies for what you provide to the grid.

Water Usage

- Turn off the taps after use, fix any leaks and take shorter showers.

- Try to only put the dishwasher and washing machine on if you have a full load. Choose to use the eco-mode as well if your appliances have this option. If you have an item you need urgently, hand wash it.

- Invest in a water butt and use this water to water your garden in the warmer months. Avoid leaving the hose running.

- Wash your car by hand with a bucket of soapy water instead of using a jet wash or a drive through car wash. If you want to use a drive through car wash, check to see if your local one recycles the water used as these are then not so bad.

- Get a water meter fitted. Again, this will help you monitor the water you are using and can also reduce your bills. If you have a water meter fitted, you will only pay for what you actually use instead of what the average household that size pays.

- Avoid baths where you can and have a shower instead. For bathing your baby, you can bath them in the sink to save water or get specific baby baths that avoid having to fill the whole bath tub.

Deforestation and Protecting Nature

Trees are one of the best chances we have to absorb some of the carbon in the atmosphere to help with global warming, so it is worrying that 78 million acres of rainforest are lost every year (Rain Tree, 2019). Not only this, but because we are destroying so much of the forest, animals are losing their habitats and this is part of the reason that more than 1 million species are now in danger of becoming extinct.

- Try to go paperless wherever possible. If paper is needed, print double sided where you can. Refuse receipts at the shops and ask for emailed copies.

- Opt for recycled paper products over virgin paper products. If anything includes wood, make sure it is from sustainable sources.

- Avoid palm oil where you can or make sure it is from RSPO certified sources.

- Plant trees! There are a few ways you can plant trees for free. For example, you can use Ecosia to search online instead of Google. Ecosia uses their advertising income to plant trees, so every search plant trees. There is also an app called TreeApp which allows you to plant a tree every day. All you have to do is answer a question or two from a sponsor.

You can also choose to shop at places that plant trees as a thank you for your custom. Did you know that Eco-Sal plants a tree for every order placed, with a charity called JUST ONE Tree?

Vegetarianism and Veganism

This section can be a little bit controversial, but I personally found it really helpful seeing the facts and figures on this subject.

There is a really good documentary on Netflix called 'Cowspiracy' (Kuhn, 2014) which talks about the effect agriculture is having on the planet. The numbers are really quite scary. For example, one of the experts made a comment on there that if we cut out all of the energy that we currently use (fuel and transport etc.), we would still break the 2030 carbon limits due to animal agriculture. Here are some of the other stats mentioned in the documentary:

- Raising livestock is 86% more destructive than fossil fuels

- 1 quarter pounder uses the same amount of water in production as showering for 2 months

- 91% of the Amazon deforestation is due to clearing land to raise livestock and grow animal feed

As you can see from these facts and figures, all three of the headings above are affected by our diet choices. By choosing to reduce our meat intake, we can help reduce CO_2 emissions, water usage and deforestation.

There is also another documentary on Netflix called Game Changers (Psihoyos, 2018) which follows several athletes who eat a plant-based diet, and it goes through the health benefits of going vegan.

If you do choose to reduce your meat and dairy intake, my main tip here would be to start small and work your way up. Start by having meat free days each week before you cut out meat altogether, and if you make the choice of going vegan, introduce vegan options slowly. It can be a little overwhelming changing everything at once and therefore is less likely to be sustainable in your life.

Fashion

We live in a time where it is frowned upon to wear the same outfit twice, and with fast-fashion companies offering clothing for pennies, it's easy for us to want to change our outfits and styles regularly. This is having a detrimental effect on the planet:

- Water usage - It can take up to 200 tons of fresh water to dye and finish one ton of fabric. Also, waste water from factories can be dumped directly into rivers, which affects the health of local people and wildlife.

- Synthetic fabrics that are used in these cheaper garments shed thousands of plastic microfibres in every wash, which end up in the sea and get consumed by marine life.

- Production of the synthetic fibres to the product itself emits a large amount of CO_2.

- To get these cheap garments, a lot of the companies outsource production to places like China and India where working standards are not what they would be here. Workers are expected to work extremely long hours for very low pay in hazardous working conditions. (Young, 2020).

To have a sustainable wardrobe, it's best to reuse what you already have first, try to fix it when it is broken, and if you then need something new or fancy a change, you can get something pre- owned. Either swap with friends and family if you have similar styles, or shop on places like Vinted or Depop.

If you have to buy new clothing, pick items made from natural fibres such as organic cotton, hemp, bamboo and wool.

CONCLUSION

Y ou did it - it's the end of the book! The tips and tricks in this book are all things that I have come across on my own personal journey to live a greener lifestyle and it is therefore not a complete list of everything you can possibly do. I hope that this has been a helpful guide to get you started, highlighting areas where you can start to make changes in your own lives.

As mentioned in the introduction, it's best to start small. Don't try to implement all of the changes in this book at once, as tempting as it is. Some things are easier to change than others, so start with the easy stuff and work your way up. I made it my challenge to make a swap every time I ran out of something and I found this worked well for me.

I hope that this book has helped to inspire you to make at least one change in your lifestyle to live greener. There is no planet-B and we need to work together to make a difference. We've got this!

Please don't hesitate to contact me if you have any further questions that aren't covered in this book. Always happy to help!

Much love.

Sally x

eco-sal@outlook.com
eco-sal.co.uk

Please note - all prices are correct at the time of release. All recipes mentioned in this book are from a Google search. There are other recipes available. Where I have mentioned a particular shop, these are just examples of ones I have come across and other stores are available.

A resource page that contains links to support this book can be found at:

eco-sal.co.uk/rp1

BIBLIOGRAPHY

A resource page that contains links to support this book can be found using this QR code or website link. Any words in green throughout the book have a corresponding link on this page

eco-sal.co.uk/rp1

Appalachain Wild. (n.d.). Retrieved from Appalachain Wild: https://www.appalachianwild.org/wands-for-wildlife.html

BBC. (2021, February 12). Retrieved from BBC: https://www.bbc.co.uk/newsround/56012612

Better Homes and Gardens. (2017, November 3). Youtube.com. Retrieved from Youtube.com: https://www.youtube.com/watch?v=bGRunDez1j4

Braun, D. M. (2010, April 16). National Geographic. Retrieved from National Geographic: https://blog.nationalgeographic.org/2010/04/16/toilet-paper-wipes-out-27000-trees-a-day/

Briggs, F. (2021, February 22). Retail Times. Retrieved from Retail Times: https://www.retailtimes.co.uk/uks-first-medicine-blister-packet-recycling-programme-launches-in-superdrug-and-independent-pharmacies/

Dixon, A. (n.d.). Mom Informed. Retrieved from Mom Informed: https://mominformed.com/how-many-wipes-and-diapers-does-a-baby-use-per-month-and-year/

Elezovic, I. (2020, July 19). Allure. Retrieved from Allure: https://www.allure.com/gallery/homemade-face-mask-recipes

Energy.gov. (2014, July 9). Retrieved from Energy.gov: https://www.energy.gov/energysaver/articles/cooking-some-energy-saving-tips

Forge Recycling. (2021). Retrieved from Forge Recycling: https://www.forgerecycling.co.uk/blog/replace-household-disposables/

Gillette Venus. (2021). Retrieved from Gillette Venus: https://gillettevenus.co.uk/en-gb/womens-shaving-guide/womens-hair-removal/disposable-razors-vs-refillable/

Green and Simple. (2021). Retrieved from Green and Simple: https://greenandsimple.co/2019/08/how-to-make-your-own-cleaning-spray

Hall, M. (2021, March 17). Business Waste. Retrieved from Business Waste: https://www.businesswaste.co.uk/300-million-toothpaste-tubes-go-to-landfill/

Hampson, L. (2019, November 28). Evening Standard. Retrieved from Evening Standard: https://www.standard.co.uk/escapist/health/how-much-do-women-spend-on-period-products- a4299531.html

Hubbub.org. (n.d.). Retrieved from Hubbub.org: https://www.hubbub.org.uk/eating-seasonally

Jo. (2006, January 6). Boobalou. Retrieved from Boobalou: https://www.boobalou.co.uk/blog/homemade-washing-up-liquid.html

Kielman, J. (n.d.). Mom 4 Real. Retrieved from Mom 4 Real: https://www.mom4real.com/3-ingredient-homemade-dish-tablets/

Kuhn, K. A. (Director). (2014). Cowspiracy [Motion Picture].

Maid Right. (2021). Retrieved from Maid Right: https://www.maidright.com/about-us/news/2017/january/3-easy-to-make-recipes-for-natural-fabric-soften/

Mauldin Group. (n.d.). Ultimate Argan Oil. Retrieved from Ultimate Argan Oil: https://www.ultimatearganoil.com/2018/08/10/using-argan-oil-on-your-hair-before-you-flat-iron/

Meredith, D. (2019, March 20). Taste of Home. Retrieved from Taste of Home: https://www.tasteofhome.com/article/50-clever-ways-to-clean-with-baking-soda/

Miller-Wilson, K. (2021). Baby.LoveToKnow. Retrieved from Baby.LoveToKnow: https://baby.lovetoknow.com/baby-care/how-many-diapers-does-baby-use-year

Minimalist Baker. (n.d.). Minimalistbaker.com. Retrieved from Minimalistbaker.com: https://minimalistbaker.com/make-oat-milk/
MP, T. R. (2020, October 1). Gov.uk. Retrieved from Gov.uk: https://www.gov.uk/government/news/start-of-ban-on-plastic-straws-stirrers-and-cotton-buds

Nystul, J. (2020, July 1). One Good THing By Jillee. Retrieved from One Good THing By Jillee: https://www.onegoodthingbyjillee.com/cleaning-with-vinegar/

Plasticoceans.org. (2021). Retrieved from Plasticoceans.org: https://plasticoceans.org/the- facts/

Price, D. (2020, June 2). Good Housekeeping. Retrieved from Good Housekeeping: https://www.goodhousekeeping.com/beauty/anti-aging/g32711085/diy-face-scrubs/

Psihoyos, L. (Director). (2018). Game Changers [Motion Picture].

Rain Tree. (2019). Retrieved from Rain Tree: https://rain-tree.com/facts.htm

Recycle Now. (n.d.). Retrieved from Recycle Now: https://www.recyclenow.com/what-to-do-with/plastic-bottles-0

Shannon. (2017, July 9). Naturally Curly. Retrieved from Naturally Curly: https://www.naturallycurly.com/curlreading/curl-products/heres-how-to-make-your-own-curl-cream

Smith, M. (2017, October 23). You Gov. Retrieved from You Gov: https://yougov.co.uk/topics/politics/articles-reports/2017/10/23/three-ten-brits-only-brush-their-teeth-once-day

Sutton, M. (2019, June 19). Good Housekeeping. Retrieved from Good Housekeeping: https://www.goodhousekeeping.com/uk/lifestyle/a28096696/bbcs-war-on-plastic- microplastics-wet-wipes/

Terracycle. (2021). Retrieved from Terracycle: https://www.terracycle.com/en-GB/brigades/marigold-uk

The Nappy Lady. (n.d.). Retrieved from The Nappy Lady: https://www.thenappylady.co.uk/news/advantages-of-cloth-nappies.html

UpCircle. (2021). Retrieved from UpCircle: https://upcirclebeauty.com/blogs/upcircle/the-step-by-step-guide-to-clearer-brighter-skin

Wells, K. (2021). Wellness Mama. Retrieved from Wellness Mama: https://wellnessmama.com/1772/natural-toothpaste/

Wen. (n.d.). Retrieved from Wen: https://www.wen.org.uk/wp-content/uploads/Fact-Sheet-Environmenstrual.pdf

Wiggly Wigglers. (2020). Retrieved from Wiggly Wigglers: https://www.wigglywigglers.co.uk/pages/the-complete-wiggly-guide-to-bokashi-composting

Young, P. (2020, August 11). Pebble Mag. Retrieved from Pebble Mag: https://pebblemag.com/magazine/living/whats-wrong-with-fast-fashion

Printed in Great Britain
by Amazon